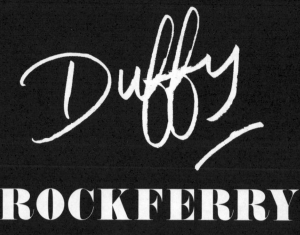

ROCKFERRY

YO-CAZ-604

Thank you to all of those involved who spent their
time making this record possible. A special thanks
to Jeannette Lee for A&R and sweet inspiration.

www.iamduffy.com

ISBN 978-1-4234-6021-3

Arranged by Olly Weeks
Edited by Lucy Holliday

Photography by Max Dodson
Original sleeve design by Studio Fury

Printed in England by Caligraving Ltd
All rights reserved

HAL•LEONARD®
CORPORATION
7777 W. BLUEMOUND RD. P.O. BOX 13819 MILWAUKEE, WI 53213

In Australia Contact:
Hal Leonard Australia Pty. Ltd.
4 Lentara Court
Cheltenham, Victoria, 3192 Australia
Email: ausadmin@halleonard.com.au

Visit Hal Leonard Online at
www.halleonard.com

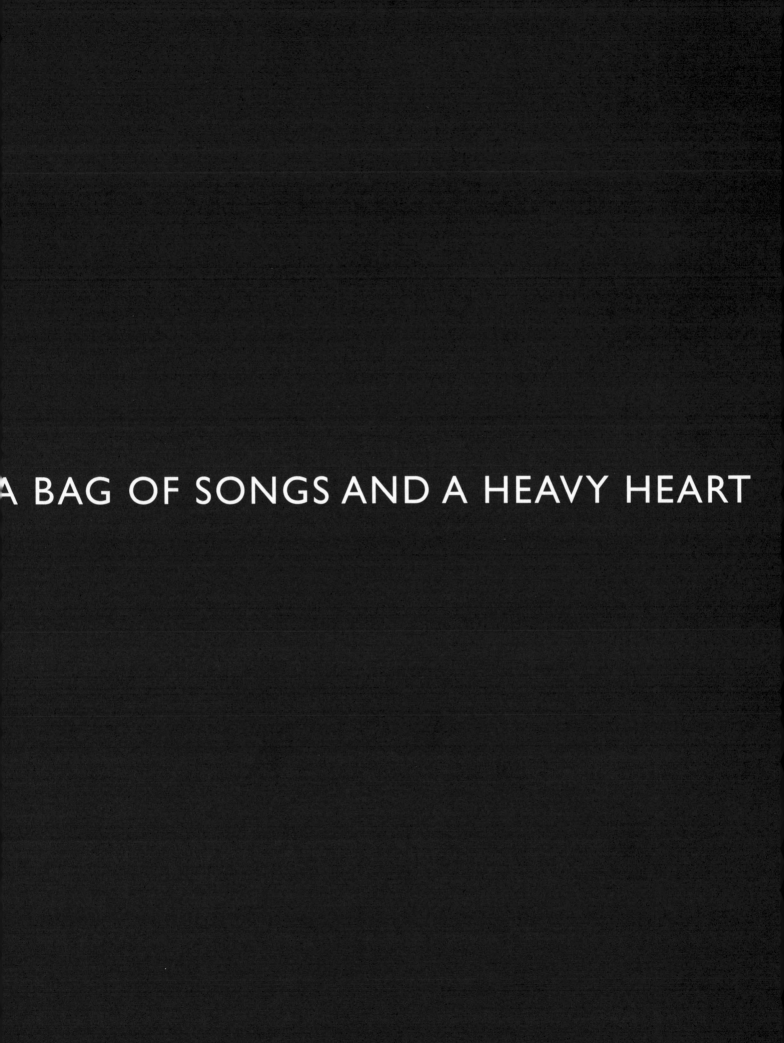

A BAG OF SONGS AND A HEAVY HEART

ROCKFERRY

Words and Music by Duffy and Bernard Butler

I'd leave my sha - dow_____ to fall___ be - hind,_____
I'd leave the stars____ to judge_____ my____ every move,_____
I'll give it all of my strength_____ and my might,_____

and I would-n't write____ to you,_____ 'cause I'm____ not that____ kind._____
I'm not go - ing to think of you___ or I'll get the blues._____
I'll__ make this deci - sion_____ win_____ all the fights._____

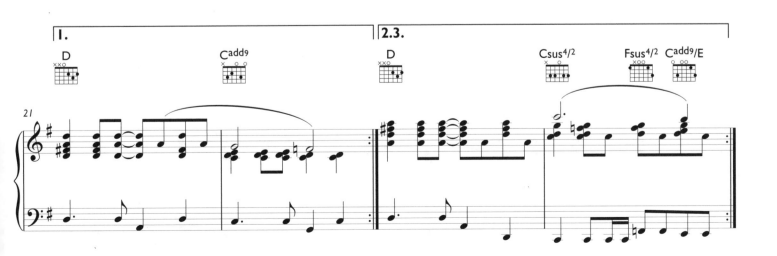

Not that kind,___ Rock - fer - ry, not that kind,

___ Rock - fer - ry, not that kind,___ Rock - fer -

Repeat ad lib. to fade

- ry, not that kind,___ Rock - fer -

PROMISE ME
YOU WON'T
STEP OUT
OF LINE...

WARWICK AVENUE

Words and Music by Duffy, Jimmy Hogarth and Eg White

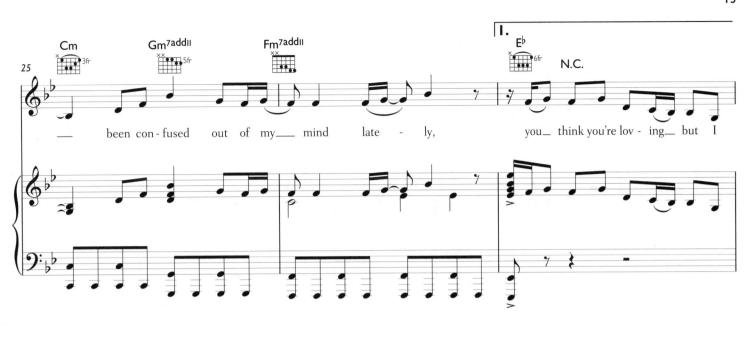

been con-fused out of my___ mind late - ly, you___ think you're lov - ing___ but I

want to___ be___ free,___ ba - by you've hurt___ me.___

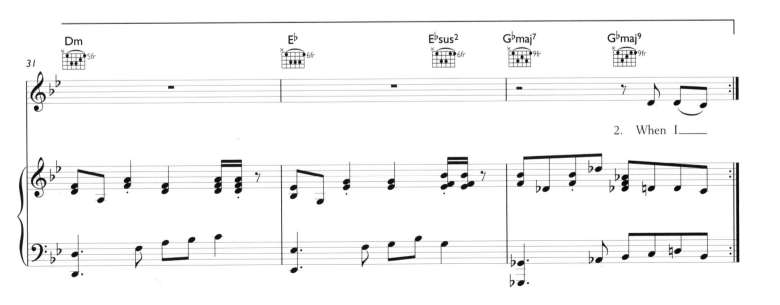

2. When I___

SERIOUS...

SERIOUS

Words and Music by Duffy and Bernard Butler

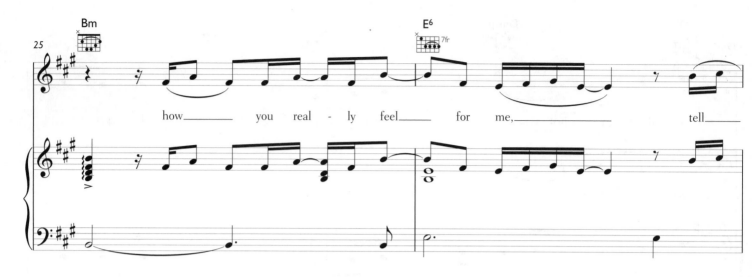

how____ you real - ly feel____ for me,_____ tell____

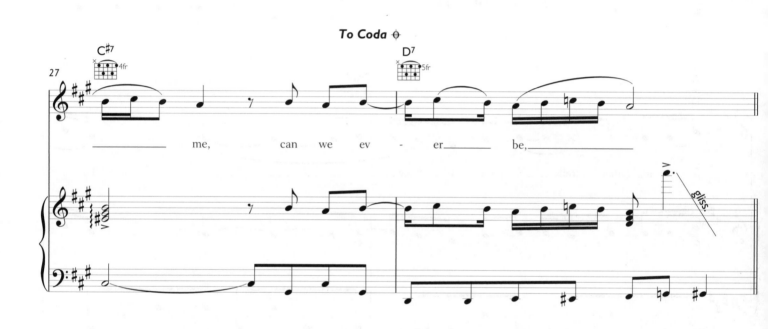

To Coda ⊕

____ me, can we ev - er____ be,____

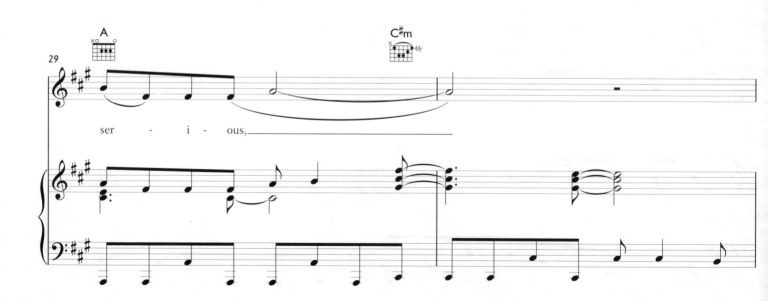

ser - i - ous,_____

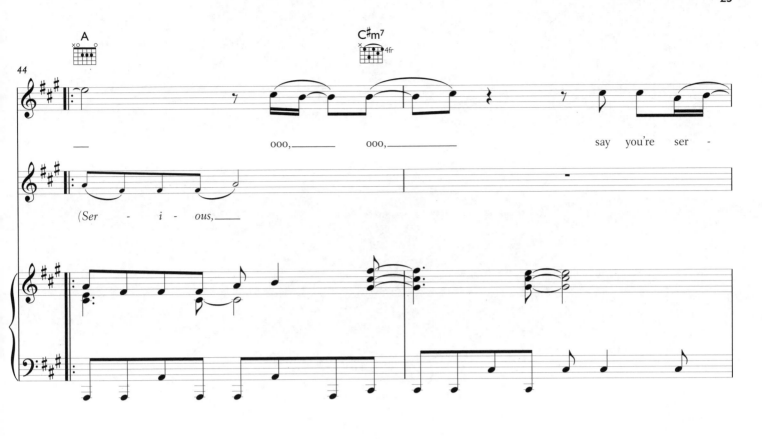

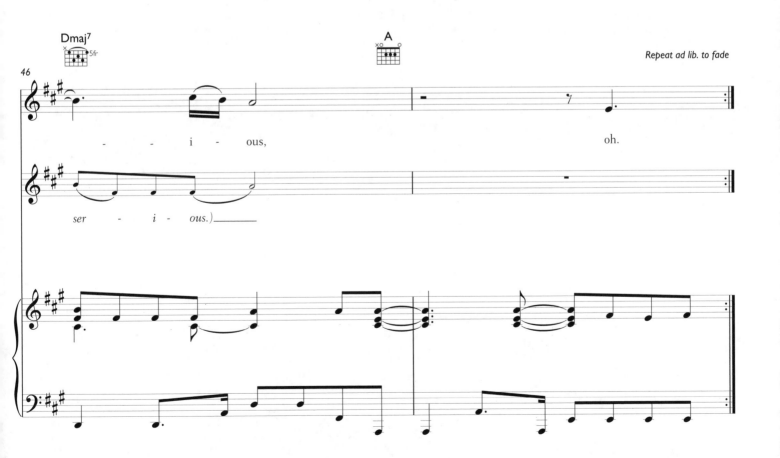

I COULDN'T CONTROL MYSELF...

STEPPING STONE

Words and Music by Duffy and Stephen Booker

No,___ I will nev -

Ne - ver be your step - ping stone,___ take it all,___

BABY
BABY
BABY
SPEND
YOUR
TIME
ON ME...

SYRUP & HONEY

Words and Music by Duffy and Bernard Butler

MY HEART WAS CLUTCHING, TO WHAT FELT RIGHT, MY HEAD WAS HOPING IT COULD PUT UP A FIGHT…

HANGING ON TOO LONG

Words and Music by Duffy, Eg White and Jimmy Hogarth

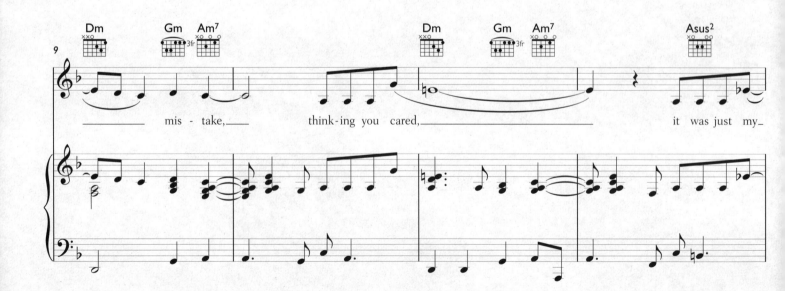

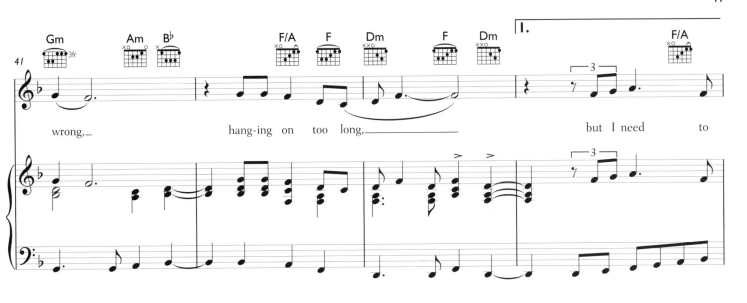

wrong,___ hang-ing on too long,_____ but I need to

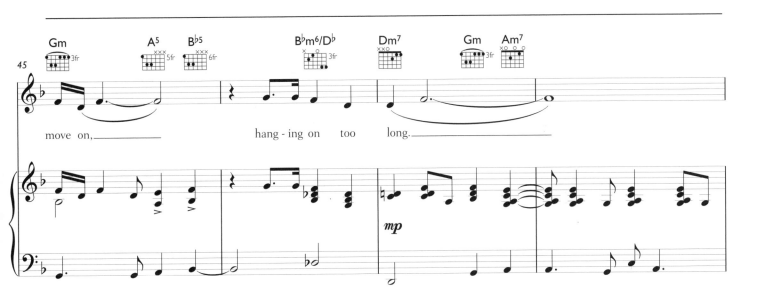

move on,_____ hang - ing on too long._____

3. I was a fool My heart_____ was clutch -

YEAH YEAH YEAH...

MERCY

Words and Music by Duffy and Stephen Booker

BUT I KNOW THAT ALL YOUR POETRY JUST COMES FROM INSECURITY...

DELAYED DEVOTION

Words and Music by Duffy, Eg White and Jimmy Hogarth

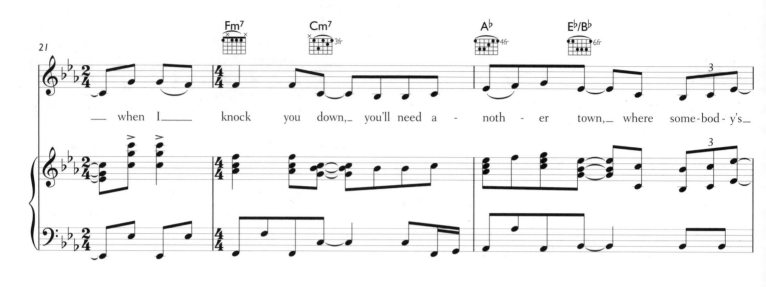

when I____ knock you down,_ you'll need a - noth - er town,_ where some-bod - y's_

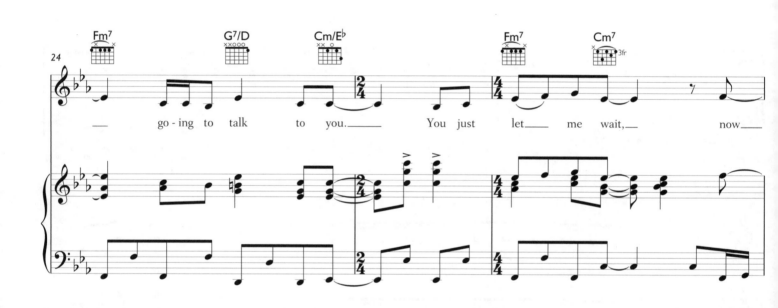

____ go - ing to talk to you.____ You just let____ me wait,____ now____

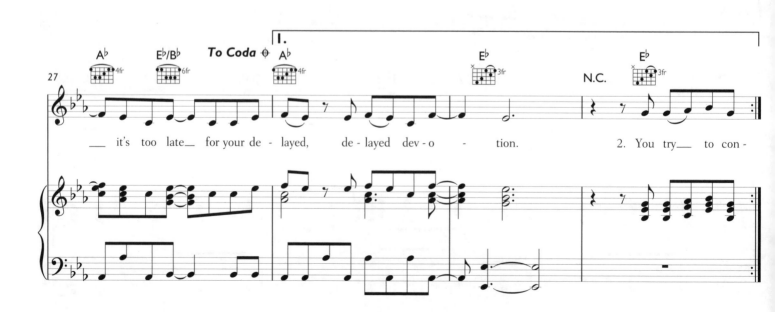

____ it's too late____ for your de - layed, de - layed dev - o - tion. 2. You try____ to con-

To Coda

DUST GATHERS ON MY STEREO
CAUSE I CAN'T BEAR TO HEAR THE RADIO . . .

I'M SCARED

Words and Music by Duffy and Jimmy Hogarth

1. The blank

(1.) ___ pa - ges of my di - a - ry___ that I have-n't touched since you left___ me, the
2. Coffee stains___ on___ your fav - 'rite book re - mind me of you___ so I can't take a look, the

(bracketed notes 2°)

fear in me___ just won't___ go a - way.___ In an in - stant   you were___

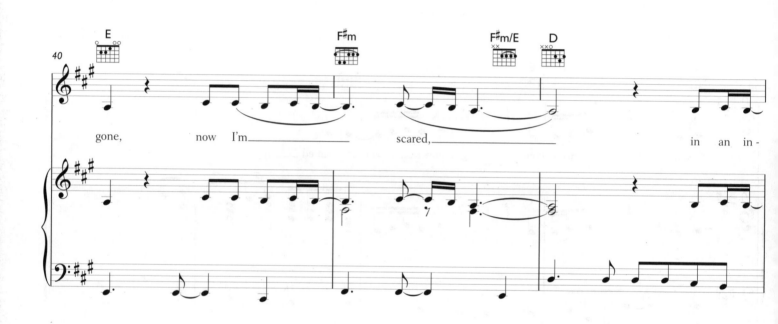

gone,   now I'm_____ scared,_____   in an in-

- stant   you were___ gone,   I'm_____ scared._____

I'M A DREAMER....

DISTANT DREAMER

Words and Music by Duffy and Bernard Butler

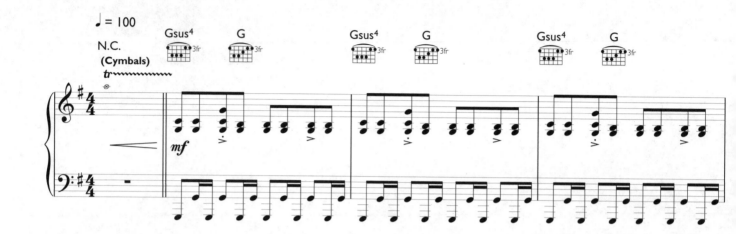

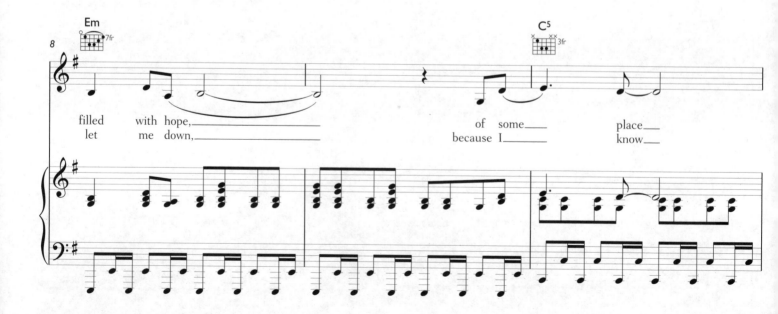

64